REBLOOM

REBLOOM

poems by

Lisa Krueger

Red Hen Press 🐔 Los Angeles

REBLOOM

Book design by Michael Vukadinovich
Cover design by Mark E. Cull

ISBN 1-888996-79-X
Library of Congress Catalog Card Number 2004096619

The City of Los Angeles Cultural Affairs Department, California
Arts Council and the Los Angeles County Arts Commission
partially support Red Hen Press.

Printed in Canada

First Edition
Red Hen Press
www.redhen.org

ACKNOWLEDGMENTS

I am grateful to the editors of the following journals or anthologies in which some of these poems have appeared or are going to appear: *Charter Oak Review, Haight Ashbury Literary Journal, Ilya's Honey, ONTHEBUS, The Paterson Literary Review, Pearl, Rattle, Shoreline: Poetry and Prose, Small Pond Literary Magazine, Syncopated City.*

To the teachers and fellow writers who reviewed my work and offered genuine encouragement: Ron Koertge, Jack Grapes, Maureen Grady, Stellasue Lee, Kate Gale.

To my friends who have taken the time to understand the life of poetry in my life, I thank you:
Gretel Stephens, Susan Regas, Maureen Grady, Melissa Johnson, Sheryl McDaniel, Cathy Tyner, Priscilla Flynn, Debbie Youngstrom, Gigi Mui-Chow, Kent and Bill Stout, Carla Schuler, Denise Dorgan, my book group.

To my dearest family. My parents: I know you are with me. Paula, Robert, Cass, Chase and Barbara: your love and support have meant so much to me. Peter, Alex and Sally, the most incredible people and children: thank you for your love, sensitivity, honesty, steadfastness. To Bob Wyman, my life partner, enduring friend, loving reader: thank you. I love you.

Contents

For my mother,
Virginia Carmichael Krueger
February 18, 1933 – September 27, 2003

I

NIGHTSCHOOL

Lydia comes to me in dreams
with ziti, mirin and white squash blossoms.
Try this, it's good for you.
Wulang, meifeizel and griotte:
some ingredients
I can't even pronounce.
*No substitutions, she says. You must
be true to the original.*

I bumble in my kitchen
until vegetables braise in earthy broths,
sauces lump and then spread.

I wear aprons everywhere.
The world is a test site for my new cuisine.
One taste and my children mind their manners.
Ecstatic strangers stop me to sample and propose.

I grow confident and bring found objects
into my kitchen. I stuff chicken with lottery tickets,
make cookies with carob and tea leaves.
Never outdo your teacher, Lydia warns,
when she samples my gold leaf salad
and faints.

But it is too late. I already
sell my basil-ruby bread on-line.
Most nights I sleep fat and happy.
Sometimes new recipes wake me up:
in the dark I bake a cake for God.

ARBOR STREET

The Year of Miscarriages, I tackled Arbor
every day. They said I could still run.
The incline was gentle at first,
then midway, an unexpected slant of street.
I wouldn't stop by then, even slow down.
I just kept going, pounding my heels
into the intractable road.

The day I saw her
she was walking downhill.
Brown eyes, olive skin, my mouth,
everything I ever wanted.
I don't remember reaching the top.

Things stopped feeling so hard after that.
I left the hill behind and jogged anywhere.
Two years later, my daughter
was just as I remembered.

Seven Hours

Answer These Questions To Decide Whether You Should Work.
Is time or money more important?
Does intellectual stimulation matter?
Can you go seven hours without talking to an adult?

My knife peels carrots and potatoes.
Skin glides into the sink.
What besides vegetables
can be pared that simple?
Maybe my table: placemats,
roast chicken and chocolate cake.

At dinner, the kids chatter
about Dad's meetings with giants.
The boys speculate in whispers.
No one asks me about my day.
They see the chicken
and the cake.

HIRED HELP

At first I can't believe my husband sends a sub.
Then it makes sense. The guy's not pretty,
and he knows how to do dishes.
He hides his nicks and scrapes with ridiculous things
like potholders and kleenex.
We work side by side.
Soon he finds a way to touch me,
that way the sub-hubbies do.

Things are looking up.
The walls of the house are clean
and don't ache anymore. The guy schleps around
in a cheery fashion, sweeping my floors
and making eye contact when I speak.
I give birth to a bundt cake.

Wow, I offer, *You're better
than the real thing.*
He hands me the monthly statement
and a rose.

GIRLFRIENDS

I put lotion on her hands,
Let's soothe the skin,
relax the muscles, she does
at home but not in the schoolyard
where girls already know who has a fat butt
and who is going to be the most popular person totally
for the rest of her life. She is six.
Her friends are six and seven.
She calls them friends, I call them
classmates. She cannot
bear to see the difference.
Six years old. Why should she?

At night in the bath
she gazes at wet plumpness,
pleads with me, *Am I fat?*
You are not. You are six and lovely, I say.
But the girls have told her, they
have given her a name, a title, a crown,
they put it on her
and because they are her friends,
she wears it.

FRIDAY ON 105.9

The Power Station gives advice
to my back seat.
If you want to be missing school,
miss school! Music is more important.
Big Boy laughs at his own jokes
in chain links. But Jamal on the line
promises to skip school.
My guys can't stand it.
Metallic *ha* whanks at our windows.

Now Big Boy pretends to be a transvestite.
That thang is pointed at me!
Laughter through the vents,
90 degree shrapnel.
Even the upholstery heats up:
by drop-off the van steams helium.
So funny, to think about missing school,
or playing with your grit,
pointing that thing
and showing the world your power.

PIGTAILS

She wants to do it herself.
The part veers left then right
in the wake of pink plastic bristles.
She gazes as though the silver window
has no relation to the brush above her head.

Each rubber band a snake
that bites its tail.
Thumb drags it around and over.
Lopsided, uneven.
Older children stamp their feet
We'll be late
but the girl in the mirror has arrived.

My Daughter Sketches Everywhere

Pad and pencil to go.
Driving her places, I try to discern
a pattern to the sound of her marks,
graphite on nubbled sheet
again and again.

Crest of scattered cadence,
hay falls in bales unfettered—
straw lisp on hardened earth.
Tang timbre of shade
in dense tones.

Then a spare breeze,
whistling at the edges,
passing through the what is not,
trailing lace of light.

Devotion

She builds a nest by our door,
then we see two tails, two small beaks,
they flit away,
humming shadows
if we stay too long.

She slumps in her nest for days
before I understand.
I see where her baby flew into the house,
a small mark of feather
on stucco. I find his body
in our cement urn.

I imagine how he fell back,
how the mother peaked over,
tilted her sorrow toward infinity.

DIAGNOSIS

His tumor will be solid,
the oncologist says,
if that's what we've got
Modern machines are so clever!
Even a resident can find it
with these things.

The radiologist smiles at me.
His eyes dilate and blink
like everything is a surprise.

Orange carpet stretches for miles down the hall.
A woman in tight pink brings me
a chair. Her platinum hair swims back
to a plastic comb in thick whisps.
She looks down, walks past me on tiptoes.
I hear her giggle in a back office.

I walk to the door, press my face
against the small blue window.
My eyes adjust, see my son's bare legs extend
beyond the partition.
The feet splay east and west.
They don't move.

Nomenclature: A Loss

What had been certitude, the assumed, became a feat,
another unexpected, bewildering twist of—what,
fate, circumstance. *Agapanthus, Coreopsis, Sweet
William*, familiar labels for regular summer blooms all but
impossible to render in an artist's mind scrambled
by cancer, neurons and synaptic clefts still young at heart
invaded by narcissistic cells, self-promotors, *glioblastoma*, bramble
of mysterious root and rhizome, vast universe of insidious veins part
of the elusive big picture, terrific growth no high-tech prune could erase,
defer even. From her chair ellipses of leaves, light on patches of blue
were a shock, she questioned the curvature of word that might embrace
such form, unfathomed weed spreading to lawn, I too
began to wonder at the silhouette of stem, fanfare of bud she found,
began to believe happiness might lie in this loss of bounds.

THE TRANQUIL BAKER AND THE TORNADO

In an effort to squash her panic
or at least avoid another Xanax,
the housewife took to baking.
For days she rolled the glossy dough
on the old board, arranged cutters
in concentric circles. Butterflies,
cows and hearts covered her counters.
In the flurry of production,
a fine dust of flour kicked up its heels
and began to dance.
A whirling dervish of white surrounded her:
she responded with a rhumba.
The attacks went away. She threw out
her cutters and spatula.
Now she teaches dance.

II

READER

After the accident, even her brow furrowed partway.
Still, she held beauty up with her delicate bones,
soft white hands. Any time of day she sat
in rehab, holding mysteries, poetry,
even cookbooks.
Words swam to her in black perfection
only halfway across a page, then fell away
to a blank void, white like light she had seen
when her car swerved. She learned to adjust books,
find the second half by moving pages just so.
Half face, half vision, searching in fluorescent light
for a glimmer of literary terrain. By end of day,
books relinquished like pillows,
she whispered her own story. The words crouched
then leaped like defiant children off a dock into a dark lake,
strong with desire to go under.

Young American Near Paris

In recovery my sister starts to practice
the French she thinks she will need.
We sing songs about Mr. Leftie,
whose spoon quakes and wobbles airborn
applesauce. *Bien sur, Bon Ami!*

We giggle about the aqua bedpan, the nurse's
fingers to remind about number two. *Mon Dieu!*
Just feel it. See our old bathroom with the ants
and the skinny-making mirror.
Easy. Compared to swallowing again.
So much pudding on the face!
Chocolate and butterscotch.
It's got to go down.

Small victories for the cowgirl who cut her own hair,
the one who flew fighter planes at recess. Small victories
I pick up piece by piece, stack, assemble.
A life, see?   Look what we made!
Tres Bien!

She returns to France without me.
They call her a drunk American,
slice up the laughter she can't control
and fry it. The dish *de jour.*

Outside Paris she thinks the man in the tunnel
tells her S and M is good for her.
She can't translate, up against the bricks like that.
She hits her head again.
Mon Dieu. Quel choix
pour une jeune fille.

Another Year Older

The employees at Fedco
will not sell my sister booze.
They saw her drag a foot,
lose her balance when she
picked up a bottle. She calls me
from a payphone at the liquor section.
They say my speech is slurred,
she says. Slurred speech. Say that
ten times.

Give me the manager, I order.
She is disabled, damnit! I shout
and whisper at the same time,
wondering if I sound drunk.
Just following code, Ma'am,
he says. *Reasonable suspicion.*
Part of our ten guidelines
to customer relations.
Anyway, she seems to be walking out.

Gwen walks all right. She treks back
to her condo, closes the door
and won't open it for seven days.
She vows never to shop at Fedco again.
We're glad they're going out of business.
Still, there is no birthday toast.
What's a party without a little wine.

BAD FRIDAY

She said it was just spring fever,
wouldn't happen again.
"The Failed Experiment—"
she didn't really mean it

(In the broken recliner,
last pack gone,
she smells her missing kitty,
sucks in her dad's voice,
If He existed,
you wouldn't be such a mess—
receiver loose in her palm,

ready to toss
Schnapps and orange pills
like candy).

On the third day they take out the tube,
thinking she can breathe
on her own.

LOCKED UNIT

The window in each room is small.
Heavy dark screen shields glass.
Light comes in like water,
thin and muddy.
She is safe here.
No sharp objects, lengths of twine or cloth,
only bare bed and veiled window.
No music.
The tune is steps in the hall of a kid
coming off a cocaine spree, heel hard
with the throb of a heart.

VISITING HOURS

Gwen has a new friend on the ward.
She seeks him out to introduce me.

Bob sits on the plaid couch by the TV
or the plastic chairs on the patio.
He and my sister won't do groups,
no way. They hang.

They dress alike, Gwen and Bob:
nicotine gloves, coffee splotch jackets.
They have their own walk:
slide, stop, hover, slide.

Bob is a good friend, my sister whispers to me,
but you know he's only half out of the bag.

She bends to tie his shoe.

FEAST

I get lonely in the kitchen, make the kids stand by
while I baste turkey and wipe waterspots off glasses.
They even offer to help—a bad sign.
I must look like that dish
balanced at the edge of the buffet.

We are an organized bunch,
yet I can't seem to stop cooking, cleaning.
Finally at 4 o'clock,
I quit. I throw my cheery apron
and sludge of wet dishtowels by the washer.
I get in the car to visit Gwen.
In the psych ward.
On the holiday.

I smell musty carpet and old coffee,
picture the common room:
game on, people in sweats on vinyl couches.
Eyes look but don't see touchdowns.
Unlit cigarettes between fingers.
Paper cups, kleenex, saltine wrappers
spread on the table,
a feast I can't prepare enough for.

Cleanup

Mind the suds Mom warns
from across the room. She sips her wine, looks away.
60 Minutes is on. Mom wants to watch,
we want to do dishes. The suds are rising,
billowing like heavenly clouds
above the old enameled sink.
My sister washes with a wonderful rhythm.
Swollen hands rotate dishes slowly, scrub
without a sponge. Pale soft arms
and blue oily plates plunge in and out of clouds.
Four red wounds on each wrist look shiny
and dull at the same time, wet
with water and soap. My eyes are wet
as clouds begin to float over the edge
and Mom says Shut it off!

Gwen At a Singles Meet and Greet

It started over appetizers, prosciutto
and melon. *Why do blonds write TGIF*
on their insoles? Toes Go In First.
It kept up with the entree, laughter
about corners in circles,
papers with *Turn this over*
on both sides.

She didn't get it. She told them
she had TBI, and they didn't get it.
Traumatic Brain Injury. It's hard
to understand sometimes.

During cheesecake and decaf
she told the one about why God made man,
because vibrators can't mow lawns,
and someone said *That is not appropriate.*
After she left, there was port and talk
of trips.

CHAT

Gwen finds herself in a room
with a man from Riverside, originally
El Salvador. She types in the color
of her eyes. She forgets to ask
if he lives alone, too. Her screen
says three times that he wants to meet her.

On Saturday morning she cooks
eggs. Her fingers arrange crescent rolls
on a new cookie sheet.
The dough is sticky, her hands
grow thick with gluten.
She leans against her window
until her back hurts and the faded Buick
parks in her slot. She turns the burner
on the eggs again.

He is at her table with the cloth
and the flowers. He sits
in her chair with the arms,
pushes the plate so that
the flower jar spills. *How stupid
are you?* he says.

One hour later she sits
at the screen, the black line
blinks for someone
to tell about the wasted eggs.

Quita in Kindergarten

I sit behind her, my fingers
tease apart the strands,
her hair so thick,
glossy from brushing at night,
one hundred strokes.
Sheaf over sheaf, brown honey
in my fingers.
She arches her neck, leans back
to adjust the tension,
nub of her green sweater
against the edge of my hand.

We do this until she goes on a long trip,
"to a better place," my mother insists.
I spend hours imagining Quita
in exotic lands. Sparkling rivers
are everywhere. The people around her
wear colorful costumes like the dolls
in her room. Her hair is unbraided,
loose and free.

SKANK

Mom calls her *Miss Melancholy*, Dad says *Big Girl*.
She locks her door with the spackled mirror,
rusted and cracked. Her hearty breasts,
thighs extend beyond the frame.

At five she dreamed of motherhood.
At fifteen she forgets dreams
as soon as she wakes up.
Mom says *Good Morning*
Miss Glass Half-empty.
Dad pinches his *Chunkster*.

Behind the school she lets them touch her,
lets them probe, push her up
against cool impassive walls,
Oh Baby, Oh Pretty Mama,
knowing full well
what they call her after.

CHORES

The day after,
she couldn't stop crying,
skipped school.
Mom came home from work
and got mad.

Whatever is eating you
is not that big. Get
over yourself.

She wiped kitchen shelves with a damp rag,
measured straight lines, cut.
Back corners didn't match.
Think about someone else
for once, Mom said.
When the bleeding stopped, she repapered,
used plain instead of floral.
That way, no one saw flaws.

Remnants

Maria cleans my floor, uses decent English
to tell how her niece back home died.
I unpack an order from on-line—
tissue and plastic peanuts float at her feet.
She smiles about her village
an hour from San Salvador
where they have no doctors.

Then she laughs: the girl was thirteen.
Her body couldn't handle birth.
The baby? She survived,
but no one wants,
como *se dice*,
a rape baby.

My latest import?
An angel, handpainted.
I place her next to the juicer,
strike a match to light her candle.
Maria sweeps.

BRIDGE MIX

My white face fades against the pane
at See's, glint of cheek, neck with nonpareils
and turtles lined up like newborns.
The clerk in radiation stripes
says *What would you like.*
The line behind me salivates
impatience. *What would you like.*
I'm your average camouflage blond in line
for a mid p.m. sweet, anything to make
the blues go, remedy that invisible
feeling, feeling invisible,
What would you like,
nothing more than reflection
mixed up with candy.
Behind me someone orders
just what she likes: nut clusters
and those little coconut beans.
What would you like,
holding up the line,
my free chocolate cherry sample
soft in my hand.
I want everything
and more.

I was running from my marriage, I thought,
running with the moon still overhead

and the sun swimming across fields
thick with corn, end of summer heavy stalk.

Asphalt stubbled the road beneath my feet.
I studied the dead frogs, fallen stars

shining on the path, smelled cow
like a sharp first breath of life,

its pungent presence a blow,
the kind that wakes the dreamer.

IV

The Unknown

Expect miracles and ye shall find them
says virtually every book on healing I encounter.
I try to buy in. Expect them everywhere,
but expect in new ways. Be open.
The urgency for a miracle being great,
change expectations of expectations.

I emerge from the shower.
A book I haven't seen in years
is by the bathmat.
You Own the Power. What's it doing there?
A miracle.
Down to the kitchen. Soda cans and pizza boxes
that were rampant with my son's friends
are gone. Disappeared.
A miracle.
The phone rings. A telemarketer thinks I should know
about a magazine available for women
going through changes, peri-, pre-, and post-.
Is this a miracle?

ICU

The curtain between his bed and my mother's
is thin, veil of this world to the next.
I don't want to live another day he writes
on a slip of paper. I see it in the space uncovered
between us. His son reads it to the family.
His wife reaches for his hand,
in the slice of air I see her smile,
comfortable in the years of love.
He reaches back.

Independence Day

Today Mother is so weak she can't sit.
She looks at me, saying nothing, I know
she wants to. Her hand falls off her lap.

Outside the window a spider weaves a tunnel web
in broad day. Summer sun parches each thread
that casts for an anchor,
clings to dusty oak leaves.

How can this happen, the heat of day,
these fragile relations unfolding?
The improbable floats with the flags.

On Mother's last day of radiation,
Alex has his braces removed.
His teeth feel slick, big.
Peter takes his driving test.
He passes but the examiner
doesn't tell him, just turns away saying,
Go to window three.
In my exhaustion
I want to lie down and cry.
Mother sits in her chair,
looks up at me with hope.

Late For Work

She tries to combat chemo
by sitting in the sun.
I leave her watching something
in the elm that arcs across the yard.
Perhaps gazing serves the psyche
at such times, coats the frayed ego
and its infinite battery of moods
with some prophylactic, elixir
to dissuade the heart.
I call out good-bye,
she does not respond.

Seurat's Picnic

At the patio table she turns each piece with care:
deliberate moves, as though the cardboard bears its own
fragility, some weight of the unknown.
From my angle at the door, I see only lonely islands,
no parts of any whole.

My mother is agile with one-hand tasks.
A slow completion of life's lists.
This jigsaw stretches before her, hour
upon leisurely hour, white gowns and dappled lawn
taking form through surprise connections
of shape and shade, pointillist promise
of what endures.

SKIN

Mid-life, I aim for comfort.
In my own skin.
Hard times: waiting for the walk sign,
seeing reflections from cars.

Mother's skin itches,
turns brown, scaly.
Like an alligator she whispers.
Don't feel that way, I say.
The doctor confides it relates
to cancer. She says she's going crazy
in the mechanical bed.

My daughter's breast buds hurt,
the "bug bite" on her chin
stings. Shirts and skirts
twist in new ways; she begs
to go naked.
Kids can, right, Mom?
She blushes.

DRESSING UP ON MY BIRTHDAY

My mother changes outfits in front of my daughter,
lets her touch the dark threads of cancer.
They gasp and giggle about my birth,
how labor was under white skillets of light,
my face a lop-sided rose.

She tells about after,
coming home to black loneliness,
washing diapers in the toilet,
waiting for later.
Now, she wishes for it all again.
My daughter helps her button.

Renditions

Chris comes to sketch my mom,
maybe paint her. She expresses
surprise: why portray a dying woman
with no hair? But she sits for him
in the thick Autumn sun.
Elm leaves crinkle around them.
Soon the tree will be bare.

Chris sketches in a large brown book
and talks to her, his Midwest tongue
soft on this heavy air.
I leave them on the patio, telling myself
the artist and model need privacy.
But what is revealed to one unencumbered
by devotion?

I wander back out to witness a graphite image
of bones and angles, what I could not see before.
His hands are slow on the paper, he is finishing a story
about his old home, the fields, the horses.
My mother appears rapt.

V

FROM THE EARTH

I watch the birds above me in my garden.
I dig while I pray for a boy who is so ill
he may die.
I kick the shovel with my heel,
push on the handle,
cut the earth at deep angles.
Soil yields to me.

Soon I step back,
grab bags of bulbs.
I begin a circular trek from the outer edge
on my knees.
I drop each bulb to its home.
Their papery sheaths come undone,
slip at angles off rounded bodies.
Some so small, even cracked and fissured.
I push dirt back over each,
pat the blanket with my hands.

BUTTERFLY BUSH

I tell her I hear that the buddleias are where butterflies
go to die. We walk out in the yard to the cluster of giants
we planted from five gallons.
All summer we watched monarchs and mourning cloaks
flit around the spikes of midnight blue and lilac.
Now we crawl under their canopy. The earth smells rank, curious.
Sprouts of geranium and grassweed scatter among snail shells
and funny pods from the Japanese iris across the way.
I squat and stare, then crawl with my eyes close to the ground.

Soon the wings appear to my daughter. Hundreds of them.
Some tattered and pale like a long lost shawl, some sharp and
strong in brilliant orange and black. Powdery clips of exotic
designs on fragile canvas. Art under a bush! There are no
bodies, only the fabric of colored scales scattered in damp dirt.

I lie on my back and rest while the wing collector works.
When I open my eyes, my daughter sits before me,
wings on her arms and shoulders. She laughs.
We gather everything and climb out. We cup our hands,
but on the walk back, some wings flutter out, and for a minute
we pretend to fly with them.

Spring Fling

Earth breathes through her mouth,
snags me from rest.
In the yard, moist coils
unfurl from tiny moons,
slurp at my dreams.
Seeds brought by wind and cats
take hold in this local
place of worship. I like to think
the cuttings need me, captive
in their cardboard huts.
My fingers itch to scruffle soft white roots,
adjust the fit to a sweet dirt home.

I toss and turn on percale with daisies
in my fertilizing dream.
I drag volumes of barnyard zest
across clumps of iris, lilies,
baby hydrangeas and early bloom
roses. Never enough,
I can't feed them what they need.

Finally I get up,
fetch my trowel and flashlight,
go out and get to work. My pajamas
drag in the dirt. By sunrise,
I am exhausted. The earth, however,
is refreshed.

Organics

In the garden some tomatoes are taut
with late summer juice, tender pulp.
Others stretch from brown vines,
diminished. Same earth,
same sun for each.
No explanations.
Only our little sciences
and big beliefs.

Digging With My Husband

to dig is the end
often. sand, silt, harbor
of worms and earthlife.
roots and rocks,
nestled in defiance,
yield to metal and wood and will.
the sslt. sslt. sslt. sound
of shovel to dirt. so good.
clean. free of what ifs and other thans.

are there techniques?
"shoe to top of spade
just so." probably
web sites somewhere.
articles ("you
and your shovel").

i don't want to know.
only to dig.

AIRBORNE

To make manifest the light outside your window,
how its memory remains—

my dark whispers but clumsy birds
in an elegant sky

soaring toward a distant muse.
They make designs I cannot perceive.

I want to start from the beginning,
the before part of knowledge and regret.

I want to change the alphabet,
build language with roots
to common divine.

I want to speak about the lucid,
how some see what is not here
better than what is,

how the lonesome dapple of absence
allows form.

BIBURY

when we went to bibury
all the old stuff fell away
like the casings
of some precious thing,
fruit, meat and flower
all at once

like a dream state
where time isn't the same
and things you say
that you mean
matter

PLANTSMAN

Late in life he cornered strangers
to brag of bamboo
as some boast of children
or dogs.
He marvelled *ad infinitum* that rhizomes
could elude fences.
A fury of roots
spread beneath his house.

The man's thing for geraniums!
Years of propagation led to shoots
in the kitchen, bathroom, driveway.
Stems grew leggy and monstrous,
stretched to a florid bloom.

Estranged family received bulbs
at Christmas, red amaryllis
in stout boxes
labelled *fragile*.

During probate, the masses of bamboo
turned thin and brown
(who knew he hand–watered?).
Geraniums popped up in odd places
like shoes and mixing bowls.

Amaryllis bulbs
discarded on patios or back walkways
bloomed again, creamy stalks,
petals white and paper-thin

FRUITION

Meryl walks my garden with me,
comments on the energy of plants,
how what I give them they return,
you can feel it. Meryl is psychic
but I think even I feel this exchange.
The afternoon breeze rolls to us
like waves in sets, lifting Meryl's
purple tent dress a bit. I see
the beauty of her soft knees
and pale calves. She reaches down
to touch some lambs' ears, smell mock orange
and nemesia with fragrance I hadn't noticed.

She tells me she used to be a gardener,
dig for hours, plant all kinds of seeds
before she became a single mother of four,
then a single mother of three. They are grown now
except for the framed six-year-old with the giggle
in her living room shrine. She could garden again.
I picture her on hands and knees, working her love
into the earth. We walk to the nectarine tree my older son
planted one year ago. *Trees respond to red*, she observes.
Tie red ribbons on the branches. You will have fruit.
In my mind, I see Meryl with red ribbons in her hair,
looping shiny crimson tendrils on branches.
I laugh, but one week later I swear
there is fruit everywhere.